BUILD
YOUR OWN WAY

Taisha Crayton

Extreme Overflow Publishing
Dacula, GA
USA

© Copyright 2017 Taisha Crayton

All rights reserved. No part of this book may be reproduced or transmitted in any form or by any means electronic or mechanical photocopying, recording or by any information storage and retrieval system without the prior written permission of the author, except for the inclusion of brief quotations in critical reviews and certain other noncommercial uses permitted by copyright law. For permission requests, contact the publisher.

Extreme Overflow
PUBLISHING
Dacula, GA
USA

Extreme Overflow Publishing
A Brand of Extreme Overflow Enterprises, Inc
P.O. Box 1811
Dacula, GA 30019

www.extremeoverflow.com
Send feedback to info@extreme-overflow-enterprises.com

Printed in the United States of America

Editing by Extreme Overflow Publishing Editors
Cover Design by Extreme Overflow Publishing

Library of Congress Cataloging-Publication Data is available for this title. ISBN: 978-0-9989351-6-4

Table of Content

Dedication	....	4
Foreword	....	7
Chapter 1	THE GIRL I KNEW	10
Chapter 2	NORMAL LIVING	14
Chapter 3	LIVE BEYOND DYSFUNCTION	28
Chapter 4	THAT'S NOT ME	35
Chapter 5	PERSEVERE	47
Chapter 6	THE JOURNEY TO BUILDING A NEW YOU	54
Chapter 7	PPE PERSONAL PROTECTION EQUIPMENT - YOUR GIFT AND YOUR DREAMS	65
Chapter 8	BUILDING VALUE SYSTEMS	75
Chapter 9	RE-DESIGN CHANGE ORDER	86
Chapter 10	THE REBUILD	91
Chapter 11	DISCOVER THE POWER OF YOU	101

Dedication

To God.... Thank you for EVERYTHING! I wouldn't be who I am today without you. I hope I am making you proud.

To my husband Dawud Sr., thank you for believing in me and encouraging me to share my story with the world. I now know how a woman should be treated; like a Queen. You are the perfect example of love, commitment and the sacrifice of a husband and father. I am truly blessed to have you and I wouldn't trade you for anything in the world. Well, except for Butter Pecan ice cream but, only the really good expensive kind. However, it wouldn't last long because I need and want you in my life. Also, you don't melt when I leave you out. You are my greatest love of all.

To my one and only daughter Shareese, thank you for saving me from myself. It was your beautiful little eyes that looked up to me that empowered me to change the direction I was headed in. You are the enhanced version of me and have exceeded all of my wildest dreams. You are a mother's mother (not really but, you think you are). I admire your strength, your smarts and your tenacity. I'm so blessed to have you.

Dedication (cont'd)

To my son Dawud Jr., you are one of the strongest young black men that I know. I am in awe of you. I am so proud of all that you have overcome and achieved. You are one fearless, educated and God-Loving warrior; a force to be reckoned with. You bring my heart so much joy!

To my son Isaiah, my miracle baby boy, your patience, sense of humor, and kindness bring healing to me and others who have lived in pain. You are God's gift to all who come in contact with you. Your voice, though soft and high like the late Michael Jackson, roars like the king of the jungle as you boldly speak out for others. I am so proud of you. Your life is full of purpose and promise. I am excited to see what God has for your future.

To my mother June Joy, my grandmother Mamie and my Grandpa Reuben, Thank you for teaching me to never give up, to never be afraid to speak up for myself, and most importantly for teaching me how to pray and trust God. You all are everything that is right about me, and everything good in this world. Life hasn't been easy for you and watching you endure your

Dedication (cont'd)

struggles taught me how I too can make it through mine. Thank you for all that you have done for me. I'll Love you Forever.

    To that little girl that I once knew, you have done well for yourself. I am so proud of the woman you have become. There were situations that I wasn't sure we would make it out of but, we did it; we survived. I promise to be true to our struggles, true to our successes and true to our potential as they all have contributed to the greatness of who we are and shall become.

    With Lots of Love,
    Taisha

Foreword

We grew up in the same neighborhood as kids but didn't know one another during that time. It wasn't until we were young professionals that we met. I was new in my career and working in an office. Taisha was a young broker seeking to build her network and was literally going door to door introducing herself. Unbeknownst 15 years later from that office meeting, we would remain great-great friends. Like most great friends, Taisha and I have our private words, moments, and "looks" that only we understand ... lol. In fact, Taisha and I have a little secret that I will share with you shortly!

Since the beginning of time, women have been silenced, sat in corners, ignored and not appreciated fully for their value - their voice, so sometimes we lose our fight - we lose our voice! Taisha always finds her voice, but not just for herself ... she finds it for you and for me! So this book is of no surprise to me. This is her voice to the world and it will change lives. Taisha is that woman, that friend, that wife, that mom and spiritual warrior that won't just call and wait to hear from you, but come knocking on your door!

Foreword (cont'd)

To get to this point in life where Taisha is, you have to be a strong woman with mindfulness and tenacity! Taisha and I have witnessed each other on our best and on our worst days. Days where we had no voice, just tears for that moment. However, as the saying goes - joy comes in the morning! As sistars, that's one thing we make sure we affirm to one another! We affirm that "joy" will soon come over the horizon.

To this day, I still cry when I hear Taisha speak professionally. This is the secret! Not tears of sadness, but of joy! It's something about listening to her strong words entwined with knowing her journey - her story, our story, the story of most women and anyone who wants better days. Taisha has that power and authority about her, which you too will come to know!

This book has been a labor of love for Taisha, I know for sure; however; all in God's timing. Word by word, line by line, Taisha has poured out her soul in this book, so get ready to move in your life by her words!

This book will move you to shift, to laugh and

Foreword (cont'd)

maybe to tears (like me). However so, be moved - embrace it as part of your journey to greatness! She is gifted in all that she touches... She is Taisha Crayton!

    Anna Marie Foster, CEO
    A Maven's World
    Connecting People. Empowering Life.

1

The Girl I Knew

Just the other day I was thinking about a little girl I knew back in the day from Dorchester Massachusetts. She lived in a six-family home on a section 8 rent voucher with her mom, sisters, and brother.

They didn't go out to play much after the street lights came on because of the neighborhood's gang violence, drug dealings, and shootings. But during the day they could be seen playing jump rope, playing with neighborhood kids, and having a blast.

The little girl's mom was on welfare and

received food stamp assistance to take care of her and her siblings. On welfare check day, the girl would take turns with her mom watching out for the mailman, named Larry. They had to be watchful because people in their neighborhood would steal the welfare check and food stamps right out of their mailbox. They had the type of assistance where you got that good government cheese.

The girl's mom didn't have a good education and was unable to find a job that paid enough to take care of her family. She was just a child herself living in the Columbia Point projects when she had the little girl. Being a teen single mother, her mom relied on the help of school teachers and her parents to raise the little girl.

After moving out of the projects, the little girl's mother had three more children and lived in poverty. During winter months, the mom didn't have enough money to buy oil to heat their apartment. To keep her and the children from freezing to death, she would turn the oven on high all day and night. And they would all sleep in the living room next to the kitchen.

I watched this little girl as she grew up. She

seemed like a pretty smart kid. In elementary school, she got honor roll and won spelling bee contests. In middle school, she was placed in the advanced academic class. By the time she reached high school, her grades weren't doing that well but she found a really great job through a job partnership her school had with Bank of Boston. I remember when she did that, "Dress for Success" program in high school.

Some kids teased her and said she looked like she was going to church. She wore 'church' clothes to school because those were the dresses that she wore when she went to church with her grandmother on Sundays.

Although they teased her about her school attire, it didn't stop her from dressing for success. What they didn't understand was this girl had no idea what success looked or felt like. All she knew was that she wanted something better than the impoverished and dysfunctional life she had.

The "Dress for Success" program gave her hope that somehow, someday, she could attain success. This little girl, now a grown woman, has achieved great success, her own way of course. Her life's journey hasn't been without challenges and she has had to demolish internal and external barriers in order to build her own path to success.

2

Normal Living

My mom gave birth to me at the young age of 16. I never met my father. My grandparents took me in and nurtured me like their own child because my mother was in no position to raise me.

At my grandparent's house, there was plenty of food and a stable and loving home environment. I was spoiled rotten as they say. My grandfather made sure I had whatever I wanted. Hence, the rotten two front teeth I had to get pulled from all the juice and candy

I had. But, boy was it worth it.

During my elementary years, the family decided that my mother was stable enough to take care of me. I belonged with her anyway. I needed to have a stronger relationship with my mother and my siblings.

Although it wasn't intentional, I felt abandoned and lost when I was uprooted from the only stable environment I knew from birth. Living with my mother, whom I did not have that mother-daughter bond with, thrusted me into a new and unfamiliar environment.

She was my mother and she wanted me with her. Although the deciding adults in the situation were not intentionally trying to harm me, I was hurt and lost. This sudden change left me feeling unwanted, alone, hopeless and abandoned.

I remember pleading with my grandmother. I begged her to let me stay with her but they thought it was in my best interest to be with my mother. Every aspect of what I knew as "family" changed for me and without notice.

This moment marked the very beginning of my identity crisis. I wasn't sure who I was anymore. I didn't have a "motherly" relationship with my mother so it was challenging to live in an environment with her. Everything was so far different than what I learned mothering should be. It wasn't long before I found myself having feelings of resentment and blame towards my mother. I never told anyone because I didn't want to hurt their feelings. It was silent but full in my heart. Deep inside I was hurting, immensely.

Before this hurt took root in my heart I had always done well in school. Eventually, I lost motivation to do well at all. As the days passed, I felt like, "What's the use? I'm not going to go far in life."

I didn't see any kind of success around me and my hope for more dwindled by the minute. The neighborhood I lived in was very poor and filled with so much crime, drugs, and violence. It was difficult not to embrace the behavior. The environment we live in becomes our normal. My mother struggled with being in dysfunctional relationships most of my childhood.

I remember one day in particular, one of her boyfriends took me to a drug house so he could do drugs. I knew what he was doing at this house because just like any kid who is told to sit down until I get back, I got up and peeked into the room he was in to see what was going on.

By the time we got back home I was afraid to tell my mother. I knew she wanted to get married and be in a relationship badly. I didn't have the heart to break her heart. I didn't want to be the cause of her not getting what she wanted or putting her in pain.

Soon enough I found a way to direct her to the needle that was hidden behind the tub. After years of struggling, she finally made the decision to end the relationship. Before this relationship, she was in a physically abusive relationship.

It seemed to be one bad relationship after another; a negative cycle of seeing my mother get hurt in one way or another. I even watched my mom get hit in the face.

I'll never forget her packing her boyfriend's clothes, kicking him out to only let him back in later. This went on for years. She would pack his clothes in big black trash bags, kick him out, then let him back in.

I remember thinking, is this how relationships are supposed to be? Geesh, what did I have to look forward to in life?

Most little girls come out of the womb playing house, dreaming of marriage, a family and the big wedding day. I was no different. However, watching the things that my mother went through right before my eyes, decreased my self-worth and self-esteem as a woman.

I felt stuck like there weren't many choices in life for black women. You graduate high school if you don't get pregnant first. Get a job, have a baby by your boyfriend, and live together. And if he can't find a job then he will sell drugs to pay the rent. That was the gist of what I felt I had to look forward to. I felt you just get what you get. I didn't have hope for what I could become. I lost the idea of what I wanted a family to look like. I didn't feel loved any longer, I just existed.

I cried and prayed to God often. I needed an answer. I didn't want to live the rest of my life like this and at times, I just wanted out of this life altogether.

I didn't really want to die. I just wanted out of the hell that I was living in. I ran away from home a couple of times but the places I went to were just as bad as my home or worse. I was totally miserable and had no escape. I had nowhere to go.

I didn't really want to leave my family. I was just hoping there was something better out there for me. I was suffering and in desperate need of relief in my life.

I met my best friend in the sixth grade, who is still my best friend today. In meeting her, I began to feel alive again and counted myself blessed. Getting to know her and her family gave me hope. To me, she had the family that I desired, a family like Cliff and Claire Huxtable from the Cosby Show.

Her parents were married and actually owned a home, which was rare for the black people in my neighborhood. Without hesitation, her parents took me in and shared family moments with me. It was hard for them not to because my best friend and I were inseparable.

I ate dinner with them, went on vacation with them and we have been like sisters since the beginning. They were a relief and escape from my own reality. I was at their house as much as I possibly could be. Although this family was wonderfully refreshing, I still struggled with my own real-life family situation. Although I saw different I was still a product of my environment. Even though I saw better and wanted better, I wasn't really sure how to attain better.

After my last year in high school, I got pregnant. I was a single unwed girl at the age of 18 pregnant by my high school boyfriend. This wasn't the ideal situation but despite the circumstances, I somehow was able to be happy about becoming a mother.

I felt like I would finally have someone that truly loved me and that I could share a bond with. I moved out of my mother's home and rented an apartment with a friend from my job.

Once I had my daughter, I decided to let my boyfriend move in with me, in hopes that we would get married and have the good life that I was beginning to believe was possible. I didn't want my daughter to grow up in a single parent home as I did. I wanted her to have much more than I ever had. I would go to the ends of the world for her.

I worked during the day and went to college nights and weekends. Her dad would say he was looking for a job but never found one. He managed to find his friends and hang out with them all night. As time passed, things began to change. He began to sleep in most days. He was no longer the driven person that I met in high school. He wasn't transitioning well into adulthood.

I remember the day that I stumbled across tiny bags with grass in it and questioned him about it. That turned into a big argument and the beginning of mental abuse. I can't say that I didn't see it coming because I did. I saw all of the signs and potential of our problems early on but, I ignored them. I ignored them because I believed that if he "loved" me then he would change for me. If he "loved" his daughter, he would change for her. I believed that I could save him.

I remember lying in bed at night thinking, "This is not the life I wanted for neither me nor my daughter." I was emotionally and mentally torn. If I gave up on the relationship then I would essentially be putting my daughter through what I went through in life, having a single parent household.

There were many times I wanted to break it off with her father but, I didn't want to break her little heart. I didn't want her to live in pain as I did. It was such a challenge for me to decide what to do.

I wanted to do the right thing as a mature adult

but all I kept thinking about was what I went through as a child. As time went on things escalated and we went from arguments and mental abuse to physical abuse.

This happened over and over again until one day I just sat and cried. I wasn't crying because of the abuse. I cried because in that moment I realized I had become my mother. I just couldn't believe I was in this abusive relationship after watching my mother deal with this over and over.

How could I be so dumb? I just knew I would be able to make smarter choices than that. I was always a smart girl, wise beyond my years. I decided long ago that I wasn't going to end up like my mother did. Yet, here I was in an abusive relationship with a man who had no plans to marry me, no job, kicking him out of my apartment, letting him back in, throwing his clothes out in a garbage bag, just like my mother did. I sat there puzzled wondering, "How did I get here?"

As a college graduate, more educated than my mother. I had a great job and a great paycheck. I had a new car and my own brand new apartment. It seemed as though I was definitely the epitome of everything

I wanted in life. That was the plan. What did I do wrong? The reality was devastating. I wanted so much more out of life for myself and for my daughter. But in that moment, I could see every dream quickly going down the drain. The longer I stayed in it, the more I lost hope. I became like a zombie. I was working and taking college courses while he was driving my nice car around doing a bunch of nothing! I paid for everything. I found out later that he was cheating on me. But, you know what I did? I stayed. How crazy is that, right? What was I thinking?

The truth of the matter is I started to believe that this was the way of life for me, a generational cycle that I was chosen to be on. My mother went through it, my grandmother went through it in her first marriage, and now I was going through it.

I began to stop believing in the dream. I was giving up on the dream of having a happy marriage, a two-parent home, buying a house with a fence and backyard that my daughter could play in with a swing set to swing on.

I felt like that type of thing just didn't exist for people that came from where I came from. I continued living life like this thinking it was the norm. I worked my job, obtained promotions, went to college and just decided to settle for what life had chosen for me.

One day I woke up very ill. I felt like I had the flu but I didn't have flu symptoms. It was very strange. My grandmother went with me to my primary care doctor. After a full examination, my doctor told me that I didn't have the flu. She then started asking me a few questions. Afterward she says, "Honey, I think you're depressed." I broke down in tears. Depressed, what? How did I get this and how do I get rid of it?

I just knew that I wanted to get rid of it. She referred me to mental health. I went directly to that department to see them because I didn't want this depression thing. The administrator told me that the office was booked and couldn't see me for another two weeks. Two weeks?

You want me to live like this for two weeks, I thought. I hadn't even eaten in two weeks. I broke down so bad in that waiting room. I didn't care who was looking at me. I mean, I was already in a mental health department. Who would care?

The doctors heard me and didn't want me to

leave. A doctor saw me right away. Looking back at it now, I was just really scared. I sat with the doctor telling him about my symptoms. He asked me a series of questions and then began to ask me about the things I was feeling.

I felt relieved to speak to someone who totally understood what I was feeling and going through. I was on medication for two weeks along with the fervent prayers of my grandmother.

I knew she loved me so much that if she could snap her fingers right then and take the pain away, she would. But, this was my battle that God needed me to work out on my own. I prayed more than I ever had in my life. I needed deliverance. During this process, I also ended the relationship with my daughter's father. I had to.

As time passed I was healed of the depression and began the course of bettering my life for me and my daughter. I took responsibility for becoming a single mother realizing that I may just have to do this all on my own but I knew one thing, she would never lack her mother's love. Although things didn't go as planned, I was determined not to allow myself nor my child to feel like victims of this environment.

So many times as women we measure our self-worth by how others feel about us or treat us. We begin to feel inferior, unwanted, unworthy, broken, lost, hopeless, and afraid amongst other feelings. We think if I were pretty enough, smart enough, smaller, bigger, happier, more supportive, etc., then just maybe I could have changed the situation. Maybe there is truth to some of it. However, none of us are perfect.

Maybe there are some things that you and I both could have done differently or better in life. Changing a person's heart or character is not in our realm of power. That is God's job. We are not God. Furthermore, in order for people to change they have to want it. You have to want it. We all have to want the change. We can beat someone over the head with it, yell at them, or threaten them to change, but change is an individual walk. You can do it collectively but it requires an individual self-commitment. We are responsible for our own actions and not those of other people.

I reconciled within myself that I do not have the authority to change anyone but myself. In spite of my mistakes and all of the things that definitely didn't go as planned in life, I was determined to get back up, dust myself off, and try again.

My love for my baby girl's life, my daughter, helped me to see the importance of creating a better and more fulfilling life for her.

I knew that in order for me to break this generational cycle that I was going to have to sacrifice and push myself beyond what I could see around me.

Just the very thought of my daughter growing up and following in 'our' footsteps of having a man with no job, experiencing verbal and physical abuse, kicking a man out and letting him in, and allowing a man to drive around in her car and cheat on her just broke my heart. I was not having that.

3

Live Beyond Dysfunction

We all have a normal way of living, including that little girl I knew. Our normal way of living is simply the environment, people, places and things that we've become accustomed to. Therefore we have a proclivity to be attracted to that which is common to us. This commonality of relationship isn't predicated on just one specific aspect of our lives but, it is the interconnection of dominant interests.

The common denominator can be things such

as pain, family lifestyle, marriage, spirituality, career paths or business endeavors.

If you have experienced abuse first hand then you are more likely to be attracted to people who have an aggressive, controlling nature and are potential abusers, if not already an abuser. This is the effect codependency has.

Codependency is a relationship where both parties individually play a role in the function of their collaborative dysfunction. They each take part in continuing the abusive cycle. The dysfunction doesn't work independently of both parties. The person being abused becomes just as damaged and dysfunctional as the abuser. In turn, the abused will see abuse as a way of feeling loved.

Over time, this little girl thought that a man hitting on a woman was a sign that he loved her. She thought he was simply fighting for what he loved. This may seem like a crazy way of thinking to some but whatever you live in is normal for you. This little girl was no different.

Her mother seemed to have a liking for aggressive men. As a child watching and hearing those things happen to her mother made her bitter towards her mother, as well as the abuser. She felt like her mother could've changed the situation if she wanted to. Her mother didn't take responsibility for the girl and her siblings into account. This abuse wasn't just happening to her, it was happening to them.

Mistakenly, the mom misjudged the magnitude of the effects that this abuse was having on her children. Although they were individuals who may have felt what happened to them had nothing to do with someone else, the truth is, we are in intimate connection and must deal with the effects of our choices. The path that her mom took in life trickled right down into the little girl's life.

As the little girl became a young adult, bitterness toward her mother and the situation she was living in grew stronger. She felt that her mother could have and should have done something to change their situation. Right before her 18th birthday, the little girl moved out of her mother's apartment. She couldn't wait to be out on her own. She wanted to be as far away as she could from all of the dysfunction. Finally, she was going to be able to make her own choices and she did just that.

She got pregnant at eighteen and had a beautiful baby girl. She found herself attracted to the same conditions of life that she despised as a little girl. She had been in a relationship where her daughter's father was verbally and physically abusive. In her early twenties, she was trying to find a way to deal with her past and present, ending up in the mental health department, diagnosed with depression.

One day, she looked in the mirror and recognized a very familiar face. She recognized the face of another young girl who moved from the small town of Ahoskie, North Carolina to the big city with her parents and two siblings. This young girl was just a child herself at the tender age of sixteen, when she gave birth to her daughter.

As an eighteen-year-old woman, this little girl looked in the mirror of her reality and saw her mother, who gave birth to her at only sixteen. She saw herself. She saw two women that didn't have the greatest start in life. She saw two women that before they were even out of their mother's womb were next in line for the generational cycle of abuse. For the first time, she saw her mother's pain through her very own pain.

She began to imagine her mother, a young girl, fifteen years old, scared and broken searching for someone to heal her deepest wounds. The deeper she looked, the more she saw the face of an abused woman, the face of a teen single mom, and the eyes of a woman who was lost in life.

Thinking about her own childhood, she burst into tears. She felt bad for herself and realized that her mother was in lots of pain, just like her. Her mother was the recipient of an abusive cycle just like she was.

She too had already experienced emotional, physical and verbal abuse with a front row seat to the horror movie she would have to fight through later in her life.

She reflected on the physical abuse she watched and verbal abuse she heard her mother go through. Because she was just a child, she wondered how and why her mother stayed in those relationships. The girl, then looking at her own situation, realized she had spent many years trying not to be like the woman she had already become, her mother.

This little girl knew that if she didn't make a change in her life, her daughter, her precious baby girl, would be next in line for this infectious cycle of sickness. She knew that in order to keep this generational cycle of abuse and dysfunction from grabbing hold to her daughter's future, she had to make big choices.

Her first choice was to break up with the abuser. Her second choice was to heal. If she didn't heal then she would only attract what was normal to her past. She had some internal barriers she needed to break down in order to experience healthy, loving relationships.

She began her journey with learning how to forgive. She was able to release the pain from her past by putting herself in her mother's shoes. It gave her the compassion to try to understand her mother's position and her limitations. Without a shadow of a doubt, she knew she had to forgive her mother.

Life is not without options. It doesn't matter where you come from. It's not how you start, it's how you finish. We all have the power of choice. This girl grew up in poverty. She never knew her dad. She had dysfunction all around her and made mistakes that could have cost her and her daughter their future. But, she made a choice. She reconciled in her heart and mind that she was going to be the one to break those cycles of poverty, abuse, and dysfunction.

This girl was taking on something that was much bigger than herself. But she believed that she was chosen for such a time as this. It was a charge on her life. She knew that pressing forward would change her life, her daughter's life, her mother's life and many generations after.

She didn't think this with an "S" on her chest like she was a "Supergirl." Oh no! She declared her destiny with her knees shaking and her voice quivering. She knew this was going to cost her something. However, the cost of doing nothing outweighed the cost of the battle that she was going into.

Thinking back on this girl, many people never thought she was as brave as she was. Even I didn't see it until I started writing this book. I never looked back to think of her. I kept moving forward. Looking back at her now, I must let her know that I am proud of her. I am proud of her choices. I am proud of her changes. I now want to make her proud of me; the grown-up woman version of herself because that girl I knew, she was me. I am that little girl. I am the woman she fought so hard to become and I'm still building on my dreams.

4

That's Not Me

Often people in relationships say that they are so different from each other. They are opposite like attracting magnets. There is some truth to this. I like butter pecan ice cream and my husband likes ice cream that has everything but the kitchen sink in it. I don't like deer hunting and just wandering in the woods, for what I'm not sure, but hey, that's what my husband loves.

Now, my husband doesn't like, what he calls, "sappy movies." I love them. My husband loves taking his time getting to places using the back roads. However, he knows that's not what I like to do and riding with me:

> "Life is a highway
> I wanna ride it all night long
> If you're going my way
> I wanna drive it all night long"
> - Rascal Flatts, 2006

We have very different family backgrounds and lived in different environments.

My husband grew up only knowing the life of having married parents in the home. He only knew the life of a person who owned a home. His parents both drove nice cars and when the children were old enough to drive, they also had vehicles.

When he gets up early in the morning to work and take care of our family, he recalls the memories of his dad doing the same thing for him.

My husband says to me often that he doesn't remember his father ever not working. His dad was a school teacher and then Assistant Headmaster. He says that even during the summer, his dad always found something to put his hands to.

My family environment was opposite of that. I lived in a few run-down apartments. I only knew life with my single mother. She did have a few long-term relationships before she got married but, by the time she was married, I was graduating high school and moved out shortly thereafter.

My mother didn't have a job. She was able to provide for us through welfare assistance and the help of my grandparents.

No one in my family owned a home; neither my mother nor my grandparents. However, it was a dream of mine. At twenty years of age, I educated myself on homeownership, credit scores, down payments, and the real estate market. By the time I was twenty-one, I had purchased my first home, a two-family duplex.

As you can see, there are varying differences in our relationship that make us opposite of one another. However, that doesn't mean we are not alike.

Webster's Dictionary defines dysfunction as an abnormal or unhealthy interpersonal behavior or interaction within a group or a family.

Remember, whatever environment you live in

becomes normal to you. People who have never been in a dysfunctional environment may not see what you see as being normal. Our dysfunctions are not normal to the rest of the world. They may seem abnormal and even crazy to the person who has never experienced a dysfunctional lifestyle.

My husband and I are opposite in some areas but there is one dominant common trait that we both share and that is, a lifestyle of dysfunction.

Dysfunctional people seldom realize the extent of their dysfunction. Just as when people with mental disabilities don't realize an impairment. It seems normal to them to scream at someone who isn't there on the train or in public while walking down the street. They have no realization of the fact that what they are doing isn't normal to a sound mind.

Codependent people are no different in terms of realizing their impairment. Some people don't understand their codependent traits until they are in their fifth or sixth failed relationship. It doesn't have to be a romantic relationship either. This codependency can also exist in a friendship.

We all like to hang out with people that have

common interests. However, in a codependent relationship, the common interest is beyond loving football, basketball, shopping or dining out.

A characteristic example of a dysfunctional friendship is where one person has a narcissistic characteristic and the other person has an altruistic characteristic. For example, the narcissist is typically the person that is very controlling and selfish. They have to be in control of every conversation. They will do things for someone just so they can hold it over the person's head (control them). They must be the center of attention. They talk badly about people to make themselves appear greater and they can be condescending and demeaning to others.

Then there is the Altruistic person. The altruistic person is typically selfless and passive. They take the background and try not to overshadow anyone. They are very helpful, polite, doesn't want any trouble and goes with the flow easily. They will put other people's needs and wants before their own needs and wants. They have no ulterior motive for helping others. They lift others up whenever they possibly can.

Looking at this relationship from the outside

view may be puzzling because, on the surface, they are such different people. However, each one of them plays a role in this dysfunctional relationship as they both need each other to exist. The narcissist needs someone to control and the altruist needs someone to help.

By the time a dysfunctional person realizes their dysfunction, they may have experienced more internal and emotional turmoil, causing further damage to the new pain they experience. They may even get fed up, not understanding their own illness, and start to isolate themselves from people in general.

Isolation can only make the matters worse if you are not in isolation for healing. Isolation will leave you with your own stinky thinking. Then, your mind is left pondering on the very things that it's familiar with, dysfunction.

If you want to have a sincere smile and live in true happiness, you have to first admit that you have some internal impairments (barriers). Not many people are willing to face their true inner being. They may not be willing to admit their wrongdoings or that they have an impairment (barrier to include illness).

People would rather blame someone else. They

will blame everyone, from their mother, their children, their co-worker, their spouse, their neighbor, their mailman, their teacher, and even their cat! They are blind to their own dysfunctions.

These same people tell stories such as, "I had to leave this job because they did this...," "I had to leave that job because they did that..." Fifteen jobs later in a ten-year span and it's everyone else's fault. You seldom will hear them say what they did wrong in the situation; whether it is in their relationships or in the workplace.

It is definitely better to blame someone else. That way, they are not left with carrying the burden of guilt, shame or sorrow, right? Wrong! You can blame someone else all you want but the truth resides in you. You may be able to fool everyone around you and get their pity to esteem your foolishness. However at night, when no one is awake, you are left alone with your own thoughts. Your truth will be buzzing in your mind like a nagging fly.

If you don't deal with the dysfunction within, your proclivities will attract you to the same damaged and broken places.

The man that my best friend and husband grew into, I love, adore, and admire so much. At the time we met, unbeknownst to me, I was still attracted to what was normal for me. I didn't realize that after all those years I still identified with this dysfunctional area of my life.

Early in our marriage, I recognized that my husband had low self- esteem. At times he displayed possessive and jealous characteristics. For some reason, he always had in his mind that I was in love with my daughter's father or wanted someone else and not him. No matter how much I told him that I loved him, he just couldn't get himself to believe it.

He would apologize but I knew there was something deeper, internally going on. He later told me about his bouts of depression, shamefulness of his past, and even his battle with thoughts of suicide. We had more in common internally than we both knew. We were attracted to what was common and what was different. Our love for one another to heal became our focus.

We recognized our dysfunctional patterns of attraction and began our path to healing together. The vast difference and redeeming quality that I love about us is that we both have a sincere love and commitment to our spiritual walk with Jesus, and because of that, we learned how to forgive quickly and love unconditionally.

We won't let each other live in the damaged areas or even let our tongues proclaim defeat. We live in the victory of not being who we were and in the promise of who we are to become.

I remember the story of a gentleman who was caught on camera stealing out of a store. The video was shown to him and afterward, the dialogue went like this:

> **Man:** Why did you show me this video?
> *Security:* Did you see what was in the video?
> **Man:** Yes, but why did you show it to me?
> *Security:* Look at the video. Who's in the video?
> **Man:** I don't know.
> *Security:* It's you.
> **Man:** That's not me.
> *Security:* (Looks at the man to see if he is being sincere and pushes the computer screen closer to the man instructing him to look.) Whose face is that?

Man: I don't know but, it's not mine.

Security: This is you. I don't know why you are acting like you can't see your face.

Man: That's not me. (Gets up to leave)

Security: You can't come back into the store again or you will be arrested.

In this story, we can simply say this man is lying, he knows it's him, and move on.

However that man could be telling the truth. That may not be him. Bear with me for a moment here. It may physically be him but, what if he was thinking in his mind that this is not the man that he knows himself to be. He may be thinking this is not me. The real 'me' is happy, fun, honest, and whole. He could have thought, you're only getting one snapshot of my life in this video and you have made such judgement to sum my life into that one 30 second video. That is not me.

I can't say for sure.

However, I would submit to you that we all should take that approach as this man did. When there is a snapshot of our lives that suggests we are damaged goods or dysfunctional, it doesn't mean that is who we are to our core. Just because someone witnessed us in a negative place, that particular snapshot of us in the very act, is not the final determination of who we are. We don't have to embrace it or proclaim it.

Maybe this gentleman was dethroning his dysfunction by saying, "That's not me!"

Yes, I'm sure he might've looked crazy to security but when you are trying to live beyond your dysfunctions, it's going to take more than just the normal way of living.

There are going to be times in our lives where we are going to have to proclaim, "That's not me!" In other words, I may have done wrong. I may have been dysfunctional at the time but I will not accept it and I will not allow anyone else to place such a final judgment on my life. People may have seen you when you were down but that doesn't mean that they have the authority to make a final judgment over your entire life. Unfortunately, that doesn't stop them from talking. You know those kinds of people that try to make you remember where you came from or what you did in the past? The people that like to belittle your successes because they knew your challenges? Do not, I repeat, do not let those kinds of people set you back into thinking that the improvement in your life does not matter. People who want to hold others back will never go far themselves. That is why they're trying to keep you back where they are. Hold your head up and declare "That's not me!" Then walk away, never looking back.

5

Persevere

There will be times in your life when no matter how hard you try; you will not be able to find a single person to help you out of the mess that you are in.

You may feel all alone and it will be hard to resist the urge to give up, but tell yourself that you have come too far to flatline. Hold on to what you believe and do not let go until the change you are seeking manifests.

Life is filled with highs and lows. Some days you will feel like you are on the mountaintop and some days you will feel like you are in the pit of the valley.

Just when you finally get through one obstacle, here comes something else. Some of life's blows will knock the wind out of you. It will leave you standing there crouched over, wondering, "What the hell just happened?" I've been there and I know that it doesn't feel good. I've cried all night long. I've sought out help and at times, I've suffered in silence. You may have also. What I've learned about life is that trouble will find you and trouble doesn't have any respect of persons. However, you have to be able to flow with the altitude of life.

An Electrocardiogram (EKG) records and prints out the activity of your heart. It is a tool doctors use to analyze the functionality of your heart to include disease, blood flow, and overall healthiness of the heart amongst other things.

The graph from the EKG shows the doctor movement of your heart. It shows when it drops and when it peaks. Life is very similar to the EKG graph. You will have some days in the valley and you will have some days on the mountaintop.

You can't control the peaks and drops in life.

It's all a part of life's process. It is not partial to any culture, financial status, education, race, religion or ethnicity. It has no respect of person.

You must be able to find HOPE every day. For the purposes of this book, we will use HOPE as an acronym. It means to Heal On Purpose Every Day. Don't go into tomorrow with today's hurt.

I've been told that "Time Heals Pain." I don't believe that to be the whole truth. If that were true, how is it that we walk around day after day or year after year vividly remembering the smells, the places, the times and the weather of some of the darkest moments of our lives?

We can hardly remember what we ate for breakfast on yesterday but pain has a way of ensuring it gets a VIP front row seat in our minds. It will replay the pain over and over again until we become mentally and emotionally damaged. I do believe as time moves on we either suppress our pain, get numb, find coping mechanisms to minimize the damage or are healed from our pain. We can't erase what happened in our past. We can't erase how we arrived into this world. We can't erase things we have said or done. We can, however, renew our minds and not allow those negative smurfs of thoughts to smother the life out of us.

There are going to be moments when if we were all honest, we want to just yell as I did my first time on a roller coaster. "Stop this ride and let me off!" We all have had something hit our lives that knocked us completely off of our feet.

If you haven't yet, like I was once told, "Keep on living baby, it happens to the best of the best!" It's all a part of life.

If you are going through a tough time right now and it seems like darkness is all around you take a deep breath and declare that you will make it.

Know that you will make it out of this situation just like you did the last situation. Trouble has an expiration date.

Live through the storm. You will survive. You have the tools in you to survive. There will be times when you step out on faith to accomplish a dream or a goal; then all hell breaks loose.

The kids start having meltdowns, the spouse can't seem to get anything right or remember anything you requested of them, your car breaks down, your account is laughing at you when you go to the ATM and you even drop your coffee just as you get to the door of the office (Now, that is some Tom-foolery right there). You needed that coffee!

Tip: A new fresh cup of coffee is key to everyone's survival. Go get a cup quick!

I know it may seem like a lot but, just breathe. As devastating as it may feel at the time, it's really not that bad. You are going to have to tap into your inner Olivia Pope and go into crisis management. You don't have to handle everything at once and guess what? It will all get taken care of at some point. It always does. Keep your priorities straight and you will make it.

They just can't all be resolved at once. You will have to make your priority list and tackle what you can when you can. You can't give everything, all of you. It's humanly, absolutely impossible.

You can survive. There were days when I thought I was so down that, "I can only go up from here!" I'm talking about days when you don't know if you're coming or going. You're just moving so you don't get stuck but you have no idea in what direction you are going.

In those times you find gems of life that you may have forgotten about or never knew you had in you. Somehow, that tragedy, that job loss, that house foreclosure, that illness or that relationship break up caused you to look in places within yourself that you hadn't even noticed existed before.

Those are the precious gems that make a superstar out of any ordinary person. It's not about whom (outer) we are more than it is about what we are made of (inner) through our life experiences. They give us the wisdom, knowledge, and testimonies to overcome any obstacle.

There are many days where I had to let my faith do the talking as I did the walking. In my time of depression, I would repeat scripture after scripture just to get the negative smurfs from having a temper tantrum in my mind.

A "negative smurf," is the negative chatter in your mind that won't allow any good vibes to enter your mind. As its name describes, a negative smurf finds any negative thing to focus on and starts to chatter.

You will have to pay close attention to what you allow in your ear gates and your eye gates. You must learn what triggers you into that negative chatter.

Our intimate space should be a place where we feel safe and secure. This space can be your home or just simply, your presence. Not everyone that says they are on your side is actually on your side. My general thinking is most people look for what's in it for them before they even think to look at how they can add value to your life.

6

The Journey to Building A New You

You may not think that you have a choice in how you end up in life but you do have a choice. Choice is your power. The decision to change YOU and the things around you is yours to make. There are things that happen to us in life that are absolutely beyond our control. There are also things in life that happen within our control. Either way, we have to work through it all if we want to better our lives and change the direction of our future.

Understand that change is not easy for anyone. However, it is one thing in life that is inevitable. People, places, and things around us change every day. We minimize change because we feel it's just to hard. Many times we are stuck in our own world of dysfunction and don't notice how powerful we have become. We must change daily.

Life is all about growth and the opportunity to progress or as some call it, succeed. In order to reach the height and depth of the success you desire, you must take some time to do a self-examination. Look within. Deal with the areas of your life that you have hidden from everyone and would even hide from yourself if you could.

You must be willing and committed to seeing this thing all the way through or you will feel like you are on a roller coaster ride that you just can't see how to get off of. When you don't deal with the hidden areas, you will misplace your emotions and begin to infect all those around you.

I'd like to introduce you to the journey of Ms. Dorothy Gale. Dorothy was the young girl in the famous movie made in the early 1900s, The Wizard of Oz.

Ms. Dorothy took a journey that many of us are on, a journey to discovering her power. Let's take a look at what we can learn from the experiences Dorothy and her friends went through on their way to see the Wizard, following the yellow brick road.

Follow The Yellow Brick Road

According to Psychologists, yellow resonates with the left side of the brain which stimulates our mental perception and liveliness.

The color yellow is known to mean sunshine, hope, and happiness. It expresses freshness, happiness, positivity, clarity, energy, optimism, and enlightenment.

Make your life more colorful. Like the color yellow, brighten up your house and your room. Put brightness all around you to help you feel your best.

There is an emotional connection that we have towards bright colors. I know for me the sunny warm days just make me feel so lively and the days that are gloomy and rainy, I really have to push that happy feeling out sometimes. I have to use my own lessons of finding ways of brightening up my day.

Create a space that is just for you. A space that

you can go to that you have placed all of those happy, passionate things in. In that space, you should be able to walk in, take a deep breath and just feel alive.

Toto, The Guiding Light

Dorothy loved Toto. He was her comfort. He was her guide. He was her friend. He was her sound mind. When she was scared, she grabbed hold of Toto. I used to think she was protecting him but, I now think that Toto was her protection. She felt safe with Toto. To me, Toto represented that guiding light, that spiritual being that helps us through the darkest journey of our lives.

During my journey, I gained a closer relationship with God. I needed him more than I have ever had before. I was going to need him to guide me through my moments of despair. He was the one I could trust because he knew what was best for me. He knew the way I would take. He knew me before I was in my mother's womb. I needed him to direct my path. When I didn't know the answers, I prayed and prayed until I received direction.

Having a guiding light that will comfort you and lead you along the way will enable you not to feel alone on your journey. You won't feel like you are in this all by yourself. You will feel safe and secure in being lead, having your steps ordered. It gives you reassurance.

The Scarecrow Needed A Brain

The Scarecrow needing a brain was a metaphor of course. It wasn't the physical brain: the portion of the vertebrate central nervous system enclosed in the skull and continuous with the spinal cord through the foramen magnum that is composed of neurons and supporting and nutritive structures (such as glia) and that integrates sensory information from inside and outside the body in controlling autonomic function (such as heartbeat and respiration), in coordinating and directing correlated motor responses, and in the process of learning, according to Merriam - Webster's dictionary.

This brain, we will think of as the mind of our intellectual state. The mind that has been damaged and therefore malfunctions. During that time of malfunction, we block out all of the emotions that make us capable of feeling. When we have been hurt over and over, our mind builds up a wall using its natural instinct to block and protect.

Being hurt and severely damaged can affect the

mind negatively. In this place of hurt, we begin to feed ourselves negative demoralizing information, stinky chatter that is.

You have to demolish those old stinky chattering negative thoughts and discover a new way of thinking. Dorothy learned that in order to take this journey she would have to renew her mind.

Replace negative thoughts with powerful, edifying, positive, and pure thoughts. Thoughts that help you get up in the morning and press your way.

Life has many ups and downs. We all experience it. However, if you are not careful with how you mentally store and ponder on these experiences, you risk your mind spiraling out of control.

Your mind can only take but so much abuse before it malfunctions. These mind malfunctions can come in the form of a nervous breakdown, depression, anxiety, insomnia, and even thoughts of suicide.

I remember well the day I thought that I had the flu. Hearing these words, "You don't have the flu, you are depressed," filled me with so many emotions. I was afraid and desperate to get better.

There is something about being desperate for change that will have you not care what people think about you. I was desperate and scared. I had to cry for help.

I ended up on medication to keep myself calm. I wasn't sleeping and hadn't eaten much beyond a couple of French fries in two weeks. I had lost weight and was looking worn down. If I wanted to be restored, I had to do something. I had to take steps toward healing.

The mind is very powerful and holds the key to open the door to a new life or new you. A fresh and renewed mind is imperative to your journey.

I had to learn how to take care of my mind. I had allowed those stinky thoughts to have temper tantrums in my mind for way too long. I never thought about what I actually thought about on a daily basis until this happened to me. I had so many negative thoughts about myself and sometimes, I even said them out loud.

Take control of your mind. Be vigilant about what you feed your mind. Be cautious about what you say that will affect how you think about you.

Whatever we think, we become.

The Tin Man Needed A Heart

Our physical heart according to dictionary.com is a hollow muscular organ that pumps the blood through our circulatory system. In other words, it keeps the blood flowing.

This is not the heart the Tin Man needed. This is not the heart that we lose when we have been hurt, broken, and damaged. The heart that the Tin Man was seeking was the heart that is our state of emotional reasoning. It is different than the mind which is our intellectual reasoning.

The heart leads with emotion; *a conscious mental reaction (such as anger or fear) subjectively experienced as strong feeling usually directed toward a specific object and typically accompanied by physiological and behavioral changes in the body, Merriam Webster's Dictionary.* The emotional ability to reason love, hope, and have passion was what the Tin man was looking for.

Life's situations can suck the hope right out of us. You will need the power of hope, love, and passion to guide you along your journey. We lose our own passion for what we love in life by focusing on our pain and our struggles. Change your focus. Think about what you are the most passionate about. Be around people that keep you laughing and enjoying life; people that can help your heart heal. You need those people in your life.

You can't afford to hand your heart on a platter to the butchers of life. Your heart needs to be free from the pain of your past. Your heart needs to heal so that it can be free to live again, to love again, and to feel the passion of your soul.

The Lion Needed Courage

The Lion believed that he needed courage because he was afraid. He felt like he didn't live up to the name, "Lion," King of the Jungle! He felt that he was a coward because he was afraid to carry out the characteristics of a Lion.

What the Lion didn't realize and what some of us don't realize, is that courage is not the absence of fear. In order to be who we are already pre-destined to be, we will be afraid sometimes. Fear will paralyze you if you let it. You have to have faith in the journey you are embarking on and let faith mobilize you.

Fear will keep you in bondage if you let it. It will keep you complacent; never taking any risk. Complacency is the enemy of success.

Fear will have you focused on what you don't have rather than what you do have. Fear will make you feel as though your weaknesses discount you from using your strengths. In order to beat fear, you're just going to have to do the darn thing. Whatever that is for you, do it. Do it afraid. Do it in the face of fear.

Remaining complacent in life and just going with the norm is not true living. It will block you from all of the great adventures and benefits of life. This is one of the reasons I do not like the saying, "Better the devil you know than the devil you don't know."

Essentially, that statement is saying that it is better to stay complacent, unhappy, fearful, or in a horrible place than to venture out. It declares that going after your dreams, your passion, following your heart, or just doing something different than you've always done, may turn out to be worse of a place than where you are.

I'll take a statement from my husband's book, Redefining Success, and say, "I made a choice one day that I didn't want to deal with any devils. Neither the ones I know nor the ones I don't know."

If you let your fears debilitate you, you will never reach your full true potential. You have too much greatness living on the inside you.

The cycles of dysfunction do not break just because you recognize them or the role you played in them. Just because you want better for yourself, that won't free you.

Many of us can relate to Dorothy and her friends in so many ways. We are on our journey to love, hope and have passion. We must remain steadfast in what we believe and committed to discovering our power and using it.

7

Personal Protection Equipment (PPE) - Your Gift and Your Dreams

Dreams are yours to follow or not to follow. You have to make sure that if you do decide to go after a dream or reach a goal, you are aware of the two types of people that have never done anything like it, and may not give you the best advice.

Everyone might not understand why you're stepping out to achieve your dreams or have your best interest at heart. There was a time my husband and I's dream was to keep the family together, keep the lights on, and put food on the table. We were well aware of the risks in starting something new, but we needed to do something different, if we wanted something different. It wasn't that we didn't already have it in us. There is just something to be said for desperation and a will to survive.

Dream Snipers

Dream snipers are people that will shoot down any vision, dream, or goal you speak of unless it is exactly what they've done in life. They will always find something negative or condescending to say and try to make you feel like you will never be able to accomplish that goal.

Dream snipers are not what one would call a "hater" per se. Although some of them are a part of the Dream Snipers membership.

Dream snipers are non-believers. They don't believe in things getting better or believe in change. They don't believe that all things are possible if you work on it. These snipers may have even had dreams of their own that were once killed by someone else.

A Dream Sniper can be the boss that says you don't measure up to this job. It can be the parent that had a rough time in life themselves and deflect their lack of accomplishments on their child. I've even witnessed a teen that was always on the honor roll say they wanted to go to school to be a lawyer, and the parent immediately stated, "Yeah right! Who has money for all that? Not me! You better get a job after high school and figure that out later."

A little while later, I pulled the parent aside and asked why she didn't think her child should go to college. After hearing her reasoning, I shared a little of my life story with her to give her some inspiration and hope. I also let her know that neither her nor her child needed to give up on their dreams because of societal limitations.

This mother believed in her child, she just didn't believe that this system/this world was set up for her black child to succeed. She wasn't intentionally trying to kill her child's dreams. However, essentially that is what she was doing.

Some people are intentionally unhelpful and discouraging. Their reasons can vary. It could be jealousy, insecurities, control, narcissism, etc. Stay clear away from them and don't take their skill lightly. They are witty and crafty in their skill.

They have been killing dreams so long that they have become experts, Special Forces. They will take your dream out faster than you can conceive it. Don't share your dreams with them unless you plan on burying them.

Dream-Nappers

Dream Nappers are people who pretend as though they are not paying attention to your dreams and goals. However, they will grab pieces of what you share with them to build their dream. They either don't have the ability to support the goals that they have set for themselves, or they are too lazy to put in the work. They think they can just grab something that's not theirs, duplicate it, and make it their own.

They befriend you just so they can get close to you and find your strength and get your secrets. The sad part for these Dream-Nappers is that they will never know what it's like to have birthed that dream.

They can only imagine the truth but don't have

firsthand knowledge of the true purpose of the dream. People can copy substance but they can never copy a true gift and calling on a person's life.

What both the dream killer and the dream napper fail to realize is you can't kill or duplicate purpose and vision. Therefore what is meant for you will never leave your life.

Protect Your Time And Your Mind

Your time and your mind are the most precious commodities here on earth. Once time is gone, you can't get it back. Choose who you spend your time with and how you spend it with them.

Essentially, what you spend your time on is buying a portion of your life from you. Determine if what you are spending your time on is worth thoughts, feelings, people, or things. Spend your time wisely.

Everything isn't worth you worrying over, Everything isn't worth crying for or losing sleep over. Not every conflict deserves a conversation. Use your mind for all of the great things that you were assigned to do on this earth.

People will try to make their issues your issues,

and they will if you let them. Some people you will be able to help. Others you will have to block mentally, and sometimes literally, to protect your time.

Protect Your Conversations

Do not get caught up in the gossip of the hour. The same people bringing gossip about someone else will have no shame in gossiping about you if they aren't already.

Conversations that don't edify anyone, get you closer to your goals, or put money in your pocket, should be dismissed. You don't have to be a part of everyone's crew, attend everyone's event, nor answer your phone for everyone.

Some things may have no impact on your heart and mind. Getting involved in matters that aren't your battle to fight is too great of a risk to your time.

You have a chance to make your life what you have always desired. Don't lose hope in the midst of the journey. You have too many great things awaiting your life and you are too close to achieving them to flatline.

Believe That You Can

In order to make it in life, you are going to have to rely on the power within you. You will accomplish that which you have in your mind to accomplish. You will need faith that reaches beyond where you are and you will need to put your feet and hands into action.

Goals aren't met by just believing that they are possible. No one ever became successful by sitting down envisioning their success. You have to put in the work. Otherwise, your dreams will go nowhere.

You can get in your car and just believe that it will take you to your destination but I guarantee that you will go nowhere if you don't put your feet and hands into action. In order to get where you are trying to go, you have to do something. You have to start the ignition button, put it in gear, and press the gas pedal.

Some people will rely on others to get them to their destination. They will go to the car and wait for someone to start it, put it in gear, and press the gas pedal. Or they just won't go anywhere.

I did a survey of people seeking to start a business or a new career. The question I asked was:

What's hindering you from following your dreams and developing your career or business?

I received various answers but was most startled by the number one answer. The number one answer was no support from family or friends. As I sat there staring at the results and reading the comments, I was amazed at how many people would let their dreams just die because other people wouldn't support them, be happy for them, or encourage them.

I have to admit, I thought about it in my Tina Turner voice, "What's people have to do with it, have to do with it?"

I interpreted the results to mean that they were afraid. They were afraid to take the leap. They were afraid to take the jump. They wanted someone to tell them that it was okay to go after your dreams and it was okay to fail.

We all fail at something, and more often than we would like to believe. It is better to have tried and failed than to have not tried at all. The lessons you learn, if you pay attention, from your failed moments are priceless. They are your very own experiences that if you take the moment to assess them, you will see how you can redirect your actions to hit your goal. Les Brown said it this way:

"The graveyard is the richest place on earth, because it is here that you will find all the hopes and dreams that were never fulfilled, the books that were never written, the songs that were never sung, the inventions that were never shared, the cures that were never discovered, all because someone was too afraid to take that first step, keep with the problem, or determined to carry out their dream."

When my husband and I started our family business, we shared what we were doing with some family and friends. There were some that encouraged us but there were also some that tried to discourage us at least until they saw how successful we had become. We received questions and comments such as:

"You think you guys know how to run a business?"
"Are you sure these people will pay you?"
"What if you don't get any work?"
"You know it's a bad economy right now?"
"You've never done that before, so do you know what you're doing?"

"What you need to do is go get you a job somewhere and get you a retirement plan and a 401K."

It may have been great advice for someone else, it just wasn't for us. From where they sat, I'm sure it made perfect sense to them.

They felt strongly about their advice because it was what they were most familiar with. What we were doing was new to them. We were a blazing trail that they didn't even know existed. Heck, we didn't even know it existed!

8

Building Value Systems

I made a decision that if I was going to maintain my new health and wealth; I needed to create a value systems.

I went through a lot of personal development, working on myself through prayer, affirmations, and reflection. It was actually, one of the best things I could have done for myself at that time. I experienced tremendous spiritual and mental growth.

I knew that I also had proclivities to certain behaviors and a willingness to always want to be helpful. In order to keep myself accountable to my goals, values, and beliefs, I needed a plan. A plan that would keep me focused and not let me waiver from what I truly desired in life.

I carefully designed a map that I now call the, "My Life My Way Plan." In this plan, I define in detail what I want and don't want in life. I also set up goals that are attainable in the short term.

When I designed this plan, I knew it had to be for people like myself. We're gifted and talented, have various skill sets but for some reason, we lose track of our goal. We end up helping on someone else's project or being the back support for someone else's dream. I'm a visionary, so at times I've even gotten lost in my own dreams. Which one am I working on right now, again?

It was so imperative that I designed this tool to keep me on target, to encourage me to keep going, and to also remind me of why I have the systems in place that I do.

I used to be friends with someone in 5 seconds. I used to lend money because I didn't want to seem like I was being heartless. Although the same people I would give my money to, wouldn't return it. They had in their mind we didn't need it. From where they sat, we were financially better off than them, so they thought this gave them the right of not keeping their agreement and returning the funds borrowed.

When I completed the, My Life My Way Plan, I had several value systems that I chose to be, "my commands" for living life.

I will share two of them with you:

- The Cost of Being in Relationship
- Money Lending Rules

The Cost of Being in Relationship

When we got back on our feet, we had a client that for the sake of privacy, I will call APA. We cleaned and renovated properties for APA. We had several clients that we actually cleaned properties for so we had a system for how we cleaned.

The challenge for us was being able to reduce our services to meet the lesser cleaning that APA was willing to pay for.

We didn't want to change our system and risk the staff doing an APA cleaning on a non-APA client's property. We proposed the better service to APA but because they had other companies that would clean for less than the price we offered, they wouldn't change their pricing structure.

After analyzing what APA was gaining and what we were losing by keeping them as a client, I gave them a 30-day notice and fired them as a client. Did my sales go down? Yes, but only until I found a client to replace them.

I did a Cost of Doing Business (CODB) analysis for every client or service. The total cost of the revenues generated for the provided service had to be greater than our total expense cost to provide the service.

If the CODB yielded a negative number or didn't have the net income percentage we expected, we knew we needed to reassess the contract.

After completing a CODB analysis on the APA company, we realized that we were losing money on this service.

It cost us more than double the payment to provide the service that they were requesting. At that kind of return, we were basically paying them to work for them. It would not have been wise for us to continue that business relationship and lose money.

The market was beginning to get saturated with small mom and pop shops that were doing what my husband and I were doing when we first started. They were doing the work themselves. They didn't have the extra expenses of salaries, office overhead, employment tax, and the many required business insurances.

This type of service and pay would be beneficial for a mom and pop shop who is just supplementing their weekly paycheck income loss. However, that wasn't our position. We gave the company notice that we could no longer provide this service.

There is a similar concept to CODB for personal relationships. We use a Cost of Being in Relationship (COBIR) analysis when building all of our personal realtionships. Too often I found myself giving people my time, my effort, my ideas, my love, and support, to only have them stab me in the back, steal from me, or even lie on me.

There were times when I gave my last to people who didn't even say, "Thank you." If you are going to have healthy relationships, you need to make conscious decisions on how you connect with others and build relationships.

You must become intentional about who you allow in your intimate space, who you spend time with, and who you share your innermost thoughts and dreams with. You too can use the Cost of Being in Relationship (COBIR) analysis to determine whether a particular relationship is a good fit for you.

In order to count the cost, you have to know the cost. The people you allow in your inner circle of friendships shouldn't be taken lightly. Those will be the people you will cry to, have embarrassing moments with, and may even tell your dirty laundry to. You can't share those moments with just anybody.

You have to know the difference between someone who you are friendly with and someone who is your friend. You can't mix the two.

A person you are friendly with is a person that you may see often, at work, at school, church, on the train, etc. You talk to them every time you see them but, your conversations are limited surface topics such as:

Friendly: What are you doing this weekend?
You: Not sure. I might go to an event but, that's up in the air. How about you?

Now here's how the same conversation may go

with your friend.

Friend: Hey girl, what are you doing this weekend?

You: Girl, I am going to this awesome event that I go to every year. I got my dress from the boutique up the street and I already lined up the makeup artist and the babysitter. If you're not doing anything, you should come.

Now, the difference is in the detail of the answer. It's in how much our information/business we truly trust the individual with.

I used to meet people and then next thing you know we were calling each other friends. Not sure how it happened. All I know is we met, we smiled, we laughed at the same joke, got each other's number and then we were friends for about 30 minutes.

For example, I know that any friends I have cannot have the following traces of being:

Needy – Have to speak with you every day.

Jealous – Gets upset if they see you were out with other people.

Create Drama – I don't do drama!

Competitive – They are always trying to

have one up on you and other people.

The synopsis of the individuals with the traits listed above require too much of my time. My time costs way too much. Therefore, I am strategic about how I utilize my time. Most of my time is committed to building up myself, my family, and my business. I don't have time to entertain and coddle the neediness and selfishness of other individuals. They may be the perfect friend for someone else but just not me. I am not the perfect fit of a friend for them either. I won't be able to meet their needs of a relationship.

Create value systems that you can hold yourself accountable to. Relationships are built on trust and broken on distrust. As you are building, you can't afford to be distracted by thirty-minute relationships. Take into consideration what a friendship will or is costing you.

If you are a person that is very productive in life, then you have a lot going on all at the same time. Therefore the cost of relationships can never outweigh the benefit. For this reason, I don't put any effort into creating an unbalanced relationship with any person. I can be cordial and friendly and it definitely doesn't mean that I don't like this individual at all. I just have learned to create value systems that keep me on target, focused, and not distracted.

A system designed to set boundaries around the structure of your life and your relationships, both personal and professional, is imperative to you meeting your dreams and goals. It will save you a lot of heartbreak, broken relationships, time, and money.

Money Lending & Giving Rules

My husband and I have a value system surrounding lending and giving away money. The system consists of these primary rules:

- We lend only what we can afford to not be returned to us, just in case it isn't returned to us.
- We lend or give money from our overflow and not out of what we need to take care of our family.
- If we lend money to someone and they don't pay it back to us when they are supposed to, isn't courteous enough to explain their position or never even make an attempt to pay us back, then we don't lend to them again.

- If we say we don't have it to give or lend, it doesn't' necessarily mean we don't actually have it in the bank. It simply means that the money we have has been claimed by a goal, a purpose, a dream and we can't risk someone not repaying the debt and losing out on what was meant to bless our family. Therefore, we don't have it.

We've had people not pay us back for money that we needed for our family and if this has happened to you, then you know that it makes the relationship very uncomfortable.

We lend with anticipation of being repaid. However, we have the understanding that the person may not pay it back. Therefore, we don't have to worry about being in a place of lack ourselves trying to be helpful to someone else and end up upset and not speaking to the person any longer.

I know that saying no to help others in need may be contrary to what you have heard throughout your life but, these are just principles we live by that have kept us from having issues in many other relationships. You can give your left arm to some people and they'll ask for your right arm too! Then, the one time you say, "No," to that person, who is buying what they want but begging for what they need, will soon move on to someone else. This same person asking to borrow funds no longer values the relationship and may even feel bitterness towards you for telling them, "No." But, you know what's best for you and your family.

Other people don't get to choose how you spend your money and anyone that is upset with you because they have a sense of entitlement to what you work hard for, sacrifice your time and sleep for, you may want to re-examine the type of relationship you have with them. This is where the COBIR Analysis will come in handy. Spend your time and energy with people who respect your value systems.

9

Redesign Change Order

Life can throw a monkey wrench in your plans from time to time. You may have to rebuild the very thing you thought you just put the finishing touches on.

It's not easy to pick up the pieces of your life after a tornado has ripped through it. The tornado of life has no respect of persons. We all have experienced something in life that when it was over, we were left wondering how we were going to get up from where we were. We were left with the challenge of picking up the pieces and building again.

After years of struggling to meet the needs of our young family, my husband and I finally felt like we were in a winning position. We were in our early 30s and both making six-figures on our jobs. We had never experienced that type of income before and felt like all of our hard work and commitment was finally starting to pay off.

We moved our family into a bigger home since we could now afford it. No more sharing of rooms for the boys. They were excited. We were too. We no longer had to deal with the bickering and the fighting over which one of them made which mess.

We had heard of this American dream but we were now finally able to live it. We had the house, the pension, 401ks, 6 months savings, the cars, the dog and the income to match.

We were in our new home for 9 months when I was laid off. Initially, it was ok because I had my husband's income and I was in the mortgage/real estate industry and knew real estate always goes up.

The mortgage originator team I worked with was picked up by a bank within 30 days of the layoff. Just like I thought, there was no need to panic. We were back in business and making money again. Well, at least for another year.

The real estate market began to take a nose dive and it was a year, almost to the date, that the first lender I was working for went bankrupt; one of the first banks to fail was the bank I worked for. I was in shock. I've never heard of a bank failing.

Once again I was laid off. The news began to pour in about banks and lenders closing their doors across the country. The unemployment rate was increasing and jobs were decreasing. I never experienced anything like this in my life. It was being reported one out of every three homes were being foreclosed on.

My husband still had his job and I filed for unemployment. The unemployment check, at 28% of my average monthly income, wasn't what we were used to but it definitely helped. We were able to pay our living expenses as I searched for a job.

Six months later my husband got laid off. That was normal for the construction industry he was in. It happened every year for a few months in the winter time. I made decision that if I was going to I decided to maintain my new health and wealth; I needed to create construction companies were going out of business and the construction industry seemed to be obsolete. With the financial crisis this country was in, everyone wanted to hold on to every dollar they had. We were online looking for jobs and couldn't find anything. The economy and the job market were so bad that we would have had to pay someone to give us a job.

I can still hear the beeping of backup sensors on the tow truck the night the bank repossessed my husband's truck. It was one of the saddest nights for us. This all seemed so surreal at the time. Just a few weeks later we also got the notice on our door that our mortgage company would be auctioning off our home.

We were in a living nightmare. This was not the dream that was sold to us, America! We were good US citizens, taxpayers, homeowners, worked hard every day, contributed to society and the community, invested in our children's education and invested in our retirement. We felt bamboozled. We were sold a dud.

There is a statement that Pastor Perry quotes, "If you're living in someone else's dream you better hope that they never wake up." In other words, the dream isn't yours. You can't control the outcome and if they wake up, your life is over. Well, we were living in America's dream and America's dream collapsed on us.

Our lights got shut off and the final notice of the foreclosure auction from the mortgage company came in the mail on the same day. Looking back, it had to be the most devastating day and the most life-changing day. With tears in both of our eyes, my husband, the King of the Crayton Empire, looked at me and said, "Honey, I don't care if we lose every material thing we own, we can live in a cardboard box, as long as we are all together."

That moment was life-changing. It was in that moment that we realized we had what was important to us. We had our dream. We had our family.

10

The Rebuild

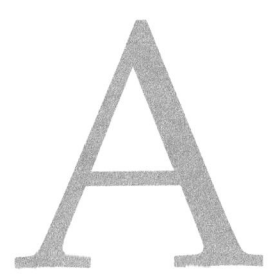s my husband and I built our business, we learned the significance and power of three meaningful factors that helped us build the business from $21 to $2 million.

These factors aren't just used for building a business but can also be used for building your career. Whether you are seeking to develop your career or your business, these three tools are powerful resources to give you leverage when building.

#1 The Power of Partnerships

Partnerships, sometimes called joint ventures, are a power tool that can be used to build momentum for your business. It can also build immediate financial and experiential muscle for your company or career.

When we were awarded a contract with a federal agency we were initially told we weren't going to get many projects for the first few months and that project would continue to increase as the stakeholders built trust in our company. However, the very first month we were awarded fifty-two assignments. Now, we did not have the bandwidth to handle fifty-two assignments in our company so we had to reach out to various networks and partner with other small firms to complete these assignments on time. Quickly, we had to identify tradespeople that would be willing to get paid when we got paid from our client which was typically within 30 days. My husband is a great connector of people. He was able to find the appropriate business partnerships with the skill set we needed. We had a group of qualified and responsible business partners.

Our partners consisted of plumbers, electricians, carpenters, general contractors, roofers, inspectors, dumpster and recycle services and flooring companies. We successfully completed all fifty-two assignments and had a satisfied customer. We would not have been able to complete those projects without our partners. We kept many of those partnerships for years.

Having those partners allowed us to grow our business revenue from $1 million - $2 million.

We never wanted to be the cliché of Jack of all trades but master of none. We stuck with what we did well and left what we didn't do well for our partnerships to handle.

We were great at property preservation and made our greatest successes in that industry. We attempted to venture out into a different market and some of those opportunities I wish we never even looked their way.

Partnerships should be a win-win for both parties involved. One of our contractor partners was with us for two years before he opened up and told me that at the time our partnership started he was struggling and almost lost his home. He once had a big business but because of the drop in the construction industry, lost his business, his cars, tools, and his home. The opportunity to partner with us came at a time when we both needed each other. The power tool of partnership goes beyond increasing revenue, an opportunity, and expanding your territory. It could mean helping someone get back on their feet and begin to pick up the broken pieces.

Not every partnership works out in your favor so you have to be mindful of whom you're partnering with. To protect you and your business it is a best practice that you start out with a contract.

A clearly laid, written, mutually agreed, signed agreement between both parties will alleviate the stress of who said what to whom and about what. There is only one understanding of the partnership and both parties. It is written and acknowledged by both through signatures.

In a written agreement everyone has a clear understanding of the partnership. Create a mutually agreeable written contract before you start mixing and mingling with anyone in business. All parties need to understand what is expected of them. Contract documentation is like car insurance. No one seems to look at it again unless something goes wrong in the relationship. The terms of the contract can be drafted with both parties best interest in mind.

#2 The Power of Negotiation

We couldn't afford to pay for dumpsters initially so we went to a local dumpster company and told them our story and negotiated a payment schedule to pay all invoices within 45 days. We did the same for the tradesmen as well, plumbers, electricians, roofers, etc. When one person said, "No," we didn't stop there. We kept going until we got to the "yes." Don't let the "No's" upset you or get your feelings down. Don't take them personal. It's business. They may not feel comfortable to you. But you don't have time to sit in a pity party. You have to keep going until you can get to your yes. Someone is going to give you a "Yes!" Remember, people have to know what's in it for them. When you are negotiating with vendors and suppliers they need assurance that their bottom line is going to increase somehow by doing this for you. You may find someone that may do it out of the kindness of their heart, but most likely not. They want to be sure they are going to get paid and that you're not trying to run a fast one.

Have referrals on hand of clients, customers,

neighbors, past employers etc. to hand them if necessary. Again don't stop until you get to the yes.

Some people are visual. You can do a diagram of what your expectation of business looks like and what you expect to give them in the next year if they can work with you on the payment end.

#3 The Power of Networking

Many people find this one of the hardest things to do, talk to people you don't know. It just seems awkward. Like, what do you say? Should you wait to see if they speak to you? What if they don't like me? Okay. Now get rid of those negative thoughts. We talked about that already.

Networking is one of the easiest things to do. How? I'm so glad you asked.

Networking is all in the presentation of the package. It's in the confidence of how you present who you are and what they are seeking.

I used to think networking was so hard and scary to be exact. Unless you were a complete extrovert, I didn't understand how anyone was comfortable intentionally going out just to talk to total and complete strangers. I didn't know what to say, what to talk to them about, or how to start the conversation. There were way too many factors to consider and no step by step guide on how to do it right.

I started off by just going to networking events and observing other people networking and talking. I'm sure I looked like a total stalker but I had to figure this thing out. One day I decided I was going to go for it. I put on a suit and put on my war paint (makeup). That's just what my mother in law calls make up. Well, I did feel like I was about to go to battle so it was pretty fitting for the occasion.

I was going to talk to the first person that gave me solid eye contact. I sipped my diet Pepsi, patted my lips with that little drink napkin and I confidently walked straight over to the woman that looked at me. She had the biggest smile on her face. We greeted each other with a handshake, stated our names and business, and then the networking began.

I really don't remember what she was talking about. I was just so happy that I had the courage to walk up to her and start talking.

She chatted for a few minutes but then I didn't

want to cling to her the entire session so I excused myself and went on a hunt for my next networking victim. Each time I would go out to network I felt better about it.

During the time that we were given the notice that the company we were working for wasn't going to have their contract renewed, we were called up by one of the agencies that I networked with often and became a member of.

The business manager informed me of an opportunity for a minority business that she thought was directly related to what my company did for business. She sent me the RFP. I didn't know what an RFP was. I had to Google it. I also didn't know the appropriate way to fill out an RFP. I almost gave up on it but I asked someone how to do it and because they had been on both sides of an RFP, awarding authority, and the vendor side, they were able to give me insight.

I filled out the RFP truthfully, with no expectation of being awarded the contract but after the RFP and an interview, we were awarded the contract. This is the contract that yielded us the $1.5 million of the company's $2 million in sales. Just think about it. If you are skipping networking, you could be missing out on $1.5 million.

There was another instance when I drove six hours from my home to go to a networking event. This event had primary contractors that I wanted to meet. These companies were actually located and operated right in my backyard but they wouldn't have given me the time of day if I just walked into their office or called them on the phone. It was my opportunity to get in front of them.

I drove out there and within the first 90 days, we were under contract for $275,000 of business.

Much of networking is mind over matter. You must know that what you are thinking someone is thinking about you, your attire, your business or your hair is probably not what they are thinking about at all. Actually, they may be wondering what you are thinking about them; their attire, their business or their hair.

In a matchmaking business networking event, companies are seeking qualified vendors to work with. If you are a diverse company-owned business then there are goals attached to government agency spending that they are always seeking diverse-owned businesses to fulfill.

If you want to grow your brand, your business cannot be the world's best-kept secret. You have to get out there, market your business and credentials.

Getting in front of your potential clients gives you and them the opportunity to get a more personal understanding of who they are going to be doing business with. Especially if you have a large contract on the line.

We all have instincts and it's hard to get a sense of the type of person you are dealing with over the phone.

Business isn't just for your client to win; it's for you to win also. Win-Win situations have the best result and yield the best return. Make sure you know who you are getting into business with.

11

Discover The Power Of You

Becoming the person you desire in your heart to be is possible. You will have good days and bad days. At times, you will have setbacks and even nightmares about your past. However, my hope is that what you have read in this book will liberate, encourage, and empower you to keep on pushing, pressing, and building towards the best version of you.

There is no person on earth that is perfect. Every one of us is flawed. Some of us have just learned how to live beyond the flaws. People who have learned to live beyond their flaws don't let what they've been through, nor any impairments, be an excuse for why they don't do or can't do what they need to, in order to contribute to their own success.

Find the time to focus on you and build you. Don't let your mind feed the broken, dysfunctional parts of you that would love to come out and play if you let them. Feed the healthy and whole parts of you; the parts that keep you grounded and with a sound mind.

Failure is Just Practice

Don't throw your hands up and quit on your dreams, your gifts or talents because your actions do not immediately yield successful results. Step out on faith and keep trying until you succeed. Don't ever let fear hold you back.

I was always afraid of guns. One day I decided that I wanted to conquer this fear. I asked my husband to take me to a shooting range for my birthday. When I first walked in, I was jumping like a jackrabbit every time someone's gun went off. It was embarrassing and humorous. Everyone could tell that I was a first-timer.

It was my turn to shoot. I got up, held that little

gun and started shooting at my target, one round after the other. I didn't have any certain goal as to where I wanted to hit on the target. I just pulled the trigger and went for it. My husband tried to direct me to do it the way he does it. But I just wasn't getting it. He gave me a different gun, a 9 millimeter and I still wasn't getting it.

I think he was beginning to feel bad for me because my aim was so off. I eventually told him to let me figure it out my way. I didn't understand how to hit the target using his techniques. I was more interested in how the weapon functioned and which one was more fitting for me. I needed to know the best way my hands held the gun, the stance that a person of my height should take to withstand the kickback, and how quickly the bullet left the chamber after I pulled the trigger. Once I had my strategy in mind, I told my husband to reload the 9 millimeter.

My husband reluctantly reloaded and handed me the 9 millimeter. He was a little nervous. He watched me miss the target and felt like I should have used the smaller gun. But I was confident in my own way. I glared across the top of the 9 millimeter, focused on my target, and fired four shots back to back. We reeled in the paper target and there it was. Four rounds directly around the center of the target. Of course, I'm bragged while my husband stared at the results in shock.

The secret is in all of my attempts, I wasn't failing. I was practicing. I was appreciating the lesson of every failed shot in order to gain the leverage I needed to get a successful shot. Failures yield practiced wins. They give you the opportunity to evaluate and improve your strategy in order to hit the target the next time. The key is doing it your way. You can't try to imitate anyone else. In order to consistently succeed, you must present your authentic self every time. Living life your own way can be quite rewarding yet remain a complex road to maneuver at times.

To successfully serve in various capacities of leadership, I have a value-add that I will leave you with. This lesson is from the good book that keeps me grounded and pressing toward the significant things in life; the Bible. This is a huge lesson because we all want to reach our targets in life and have people understand where we are coming from but, the lesson I value comes from James 1:19, "be quick to listen, slow to speak and slow to become angry." I've also learned from Matthew 10:16, "to be wise as a serpent, yet as harmless as a dove."

Remember that change takes time so don't be hard on yourself if you have a setback or if you still cry when you think of certain situations in your life. Do what you can do and let God handle the rest. You are human and unfortunately, there are things in life so damaging that they will forever peek into your heart and mind. Here are 10 key factors you can use to remind yourself of as you discover your power and build your own way.

1. Don't get stuck in your past, it will keep you from creating a brighter future.
2. Protect you! You are your #1 Resource.
3. Don't ever give up.
4. Be flexible to change. Life happens.
5. You are not a failure; you are a learner.
6. You are always one 'No' away from 'Yes.'
7. Focus and deliver on the basis of your own style, gifts, talents, and experiences
8. It's okay to ask for help. We all need help sometimes.

9. Re-evaluate and improve upon the methods that best fit you.

10. Celebrate every win; big or small.

Every morning you wake is a brand new opportunity to take steps towards a better you. Be committed to love, smile, learn, play, run, dream, sing, and laugh again. Be committed to living your best life as you build it your way.

www.ingramcontent.com/pod-product-compliance
Lightning Source LLC
LaVergne TN
LVHW051507070426
835507LV00022B/2969